TOWN HALL
BIRMINGHAM

A HISTORY IN PICTURES

1845: The Town Hall from Paradise Street

FIONA FRASER & LYNDON JENKINS

Supported by The Patrick Trust

Text by Lyndon Jenkins

Designed by Tina Ranft

First published 2007
The Boydell Press, Woodbridge

ISBN 978-1-84383-381-9 Hardback
ISBN 978-1-84383-349-9 Paperback

Published on behalf of Performances Birmingham Limited
Symphony Hall, Broad Street, Birmingham, B1 2EA, UK
Registered Charity No. 1053937. Registered in England No. 3169600.
www.thsh.co.uk

The Boydell Press is an imprint of Boydell & Brewer Ltd
PO Box 9, Woodbridge, Suffolk, IP12 3DF, UK *and of*
Boydell & Brewer Inc.
668 Mt Hope Avenue, Rochester, NY 14620, USA
www.boydellandbrewer.com

Cover image: Mike Gutteridge

A CiP catalogue record for this book is available from the British Library
This publication is printed on acid-free paper

Printed in Great Britain by Ashford Colour Press

Town Hall restoration funded by:

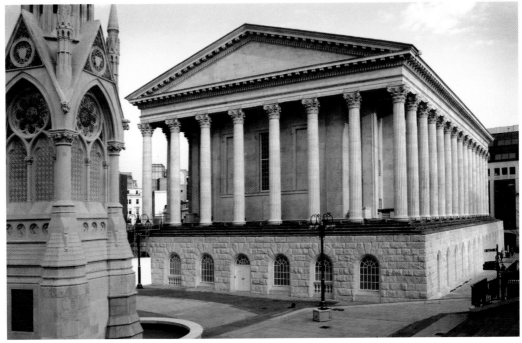

The newly restored Town Hall in 2007

CONTENTS

Birmingham Post & Mail Ltd

IT GIVES ME THE GREATEST PLEASURE to be able to support, through the
Patrick Trust, this fascinating book about the history of Town Hall, Birmingham.

Charles Dickens, one of many distinguished figures featured in these pages,
frequently expressed his admiration for Birmingham as a city of commerce,
invention and, above all, education. In one of his first speeches after the
opening of the historic building commemorated in this book he singled out the
public spirit he found in Birmingham, which he felt was based 'upon the name
and fame of its capitalists and working men; upon the importance of its
merchants and manufacturers; upon the skill and intelligence of its artisans; and
the increasing knowledge of all portions of the community'. The last was a
favourite cause, and it later led Dickens to rally support for the founding of
what became the Birmingham & Midland Institute, equating it in importance
with the Town Hall as 'an admirable educational institution', partly because of
the way in which the latter's concerts were for everybody and did not neglect
'the work-people'.

Dickens was quite right, of course, because although the Town Hall became
in later periods a building strongly associated in the public mind with
entertainment, it was from the start intended equally to answer the needs of a
meeting-place that would provide a focus for debates on every possible subject,
something of which Dickens certainly approved. Today, when the clamour for
public debates has very largely subsided, the great Town Hall is nevertheless
emerging once again as the all-purpose building that it always was.
Magnificently restored, it can rarely have looked more handsome at any time
since its opening 173 years ago – 56 years prior to my great-grandfather settling
in Birmingham in 1890.

Together with every citizen I welcome its return, and I am delighted to be
associated with this publication recalling its proud history.

J Alexander Patrick

Kings Norton, August 2007

INTRODUCTION & ACKNOWLEDGEMENTS

Birmingham's Town Hall has been witness to numberless events and occasions of every kind and variety during its 173-year history – *but only one previous re-opening.* That was in 1927, after closure for internal structural alterations. It seems appropriate, therefore, that the occasion of its second rebirth, 80 years later and following an even more extensive refurbishment under the leadership of Birmingham City Council, should be marked in some way. That is the intention of this book. It is not an attempt at a history of this grand old building, now revitalised and renewed two centuries distant from that which saw it built, but rather to convey an impression by means of an assemblage of photographs of the multifarious activities that the Hall has accommodated over all these years. Its preparation has naturally depended upon what material the various archives consulted have been able to yield, but it is to be hoped that readers will feel that we have succeeded in our aim of assembling at least a representative number of images, and that they will obtain enjoyment from viewing these pages.

Among the archives consulted were Birmingham Central Library's Designated Collections and those of the Birmingham Museum and Art Gallery: we should like to thank Patrick Baird, Alison Smith, Richard Allbutt and Jo-Ann Curtis for arranging permissions. We are especially indebted to the Birmingham Post and its Editor, Marc Reeves, who allowed us free run of the Birmingham Post & Mail's photographic library, which was crucially helpful in locating pictures of happenings in the Town Hall over the last half-century that would hardly be available from any other source; at the Birmingham Post we should like to thank Adam Fradgley, Regional Picture Editor, and Anna Burke, Librarian, for their patient assistance. Also at the Birmingham Post we should like to acknowledge Terry Grimley, Arts Editor, together with John Gough (former Head of Music Services, Birmingham Libraries): both placed their own long experience of Birmingham's history at the disposal of our small editorial committee, and this has been invaluable. May we also acknowledge willing assistance from Beresford King-Smith (CBSO Archivist) and from Jim Simpson and Alan Wood, who provided some superb examples from their extensive collections of musical pictures; Bev Bevan, for kindly locating some material personal to him; Sir Bernard Zissman for some intricate guidance; Betty Milne (Town Hall Manager 1979–93) and Mary Daniels, who allowed access to items from their private collections. Among other individuals we should like to record our thanks to Mike Gutteridge, Laurie Hornsby and Gerard Dobbin; also to the Birmingham Civic Society; the City of Birmingham Choir and the Birmingham Choral Union. Pictures of the restoration of the Town Hall have been provided by Wates Construction.

Fiona Fraser
Lyndon Jenkins

CHAPTER ONE

1834–1912

A HALL FOR ALL
PURPOSES

WILLIAM BOLTON, Secretary.

TO ARCHITECTS.

THE Commissioners of the Birmingham Street Act having determined to erect a TOWN HALL, on a site recently purchased by them in Paradise-street and Congreve-street, are desirous of receiving Plans, Specifications, and Estimates of the proposed Building, which is to be used for the Musical Festivals as well as for the general purposes of a Town Hall.

A premium of £100 will be paid to the Architect who shall furnish the Plan most approved by the Commissioners, and £60 and £40 to the respective parties who shall supply the second and third best, with the understanding that such Plans are to be at the disposal of the Commissioners.

A Ground Plot of the Land, shewing its extent, form, and level, may be obtained by application to Messrs. Arnold and Haines, Solicitors, Birmingham, of whom also further particulars may be had.

The Plans, Specifications, and Estimates must be delivered to us, sealed up, and addressed to " The Town Hall Committee," on or before the 1st day of February next.

By order of the Commissioners,
ARNOLD and HAINES, Clerks.
Birmingham, Dec. 2, 1830.

TO BUILDERS AND OTHERS.

THERE HAD BEEN TALK of a town hall for Birmingham 'in which to hold public and town meetings, concerts and other entertainments' for a few years, but this was the announcement that finally set it in motion. Of the designs submitted, one based on the Roman temple of Castor and Pollux by 27-year old Joseph Hansom was selected, and the first brick laid in April 1832. Hansom – later the inventor of the horse-drawn cab named after him – soon dropped out of the picture: he had unwisely allowed himself to take on all financial responsibility for the project and, when costs far exceeded estimates, he was bankrupted. His name is nevertheless properly recorded both outside and inside the building. The Town Hall, complete with a fine organ financed by a special appeal, was made ready to stage its opening event in October 1834, though actual completion of the whole building was not to be finally achieved until 1851.

Among those looking on with satisfaction and pleasure must have been Joseph Moore, chairman of the Birmingham Triennial Festivals organising committee since 1802. His tireless advocacy of the need for a new hall meant that the festivals, which had been held in cramped conditions for almost 60 years, at last had a setting worthy of them and he could begin to realise some ambitious plans intended to make them unrivalled in England. No sooner was the first festival over than he travelled to Germany in the hope of persuading one of the great composers of the day, Felix Mendelssohn, to participate in the next, due in 1837. He was successful and Mendelssohn's music, his playing and conducting took Birmingham by storm. The next few festivals were modelled around him, the crowning glory reached with the presentation in 1846 of an oratorio he composed especially for Birmingham. That work, *Elijah,* truly placed Birmingham on the musical map, and crowned Moore's ambitious aims for the festivals. It was just in time: Mendelssohn, who was persuaded back in 1847 to repeat his triumph by conducting *Elijah* again, died later that year at only 38; the next year Birmingham mounted a special memorial festival in his honour.

Although the Town Hall's history during the next 78 years can be conveniently marked out by the three-yearly festivals up to the last in 1912, they were far from being the only musical events there. From the moment in 1838 when Johann Strauss I (founder of the Strauss dynasty and composer of the *Radetzky March*) arrived with his orchestra, virtually every international performer appeared there. Especially popular were great singers such as Jenny Lind, Nellie Melba and Adelina Patti in the early years, and John McCormack, Luisa Tetrazzini and Clara Butt in later periods. Louis Jullien from Paris brought promenade concerts with a French flavour, violin virtuosi such as Wieniawski, Joachim and Sarasate and a plethora of pianists ranging from Schumann's widow Clara and Adelina de Lara to Paderewski and Busoni all made their way to Birmingham. Grieg gave one of his last recitals of his music in Birmingham (1897). Orchestral music was mostly provided by *ad hoc* groups made up of local players and others from outside, especially after 1873 when Stockley, the Triennial Festival's chorus-master, launched a concert series that ran for 25 years: in 1882 he recruited to his ranks a young Worcester violinist named Edward Elgar, and gave a first hearing to some of the budding composer's compositions. Stockley's concerts were supplemented by visits from the Hallé, Britain's oldest orchestra, with its founder-conductor Charles Hallé, followed in later years by ensembles newly-formed elsewhere such as the Queen's Hall and London Symphony orchestras.

Joseph Aloysius Hansom (1803–1882)

Aside from musical and associated entertainments, the new hall quickly began to fulfil its intended function as an important meeting-place. Political gatherings – a significant number addressed by Joseph Chamberlain (1836–1914) who was so intimately bound up with the development of the city – rubbed shoulders with hundreds of lectures, campaign speeches and addresses on every imaginable topic from education and religion to slavery and colonial tariffs. Quite one of the most notorious occasions is remembered from 1901 when David Lloyd George's address opposing the Boer War caused a full-scale riot; one man was killed in the melée, and the unpopular orator had to be smuggled out of the Town Hall disguised as a policeman. Less controversial was the meeting that led to the building of the Midland Institute – Charles Dickens read 'A Christmas Carol' to a packed audience in support of it, and subsequently delivered his inaugural presidential address in 1869.

The Christadelphian Church in Birmingham which was established in 1864 attracted huge numbers of people to its meetings, as did the Independent Order of Rechabites. Important national organisations such as the British Association chose Birmingham for their gatherings, as did much later the political parties for their annual conferences; the Justices' Sessions were occasionally held in the Hall, and banquets, dinners, receptions, soirées and balls proliferated. Special entertainments were put on for 'The city's policemen, postmen, firemen and their families', and in aid of 'Aged and Distressed Housekeepers'. And at last Birmingham had a Hall suitable for entertaining royalty, which was especially important after it attained its charter as a city in 1889: Queen Victoria's visits during her long reign became scenes of lavish spectacle. As late as the 1880s the Hall's seating-plans show accommodation for an astonishing 2083 people: this was mostly on benches, and in 1891 came the announcement that they would be replaced by stuffed armchairs, (so) 'greatly increasing the comfort of the audience.'

In among all the hugely varied mix of education and entertainment the Birmingham Festivals came around every three years. The composer Arthur Sullivan good-naturedly chaffed musical Birmingham for being 'like a huge boa constrictor that gorged itself every three years and fasted in between', but it was the very regularity of the festivals that helped establish a supremacy for them that was not to be denied. After Mendelssohn the autocratic Italian composer Michael Costa was in charge for the next 40 years, though it was in some ways a barren period because the new native works that were presented in preference to those of established composers mostly proved unworthy and, in retrospect, the Costa period can be seen to have stifled progress. All that changed in 1885 with the arrival of the cosmopolitan Hans Richter, when once again the musical offerings of composers such as Grieg, Gounod, Dvořák and Sibelius, stimulated by the composers' personal appearances in Birmingham, elevated the festivals above all rivals.

Hansom cabs in
the moonlight

While Birmingham was no doubt proud to have such illustrious personages in
its midst, the composers were pretty impressed with Birmingham too: 'I'm here in
this immense industrial city', wrote Antonin Dvořák to his family in Prague, 'where
they make excellent knives, scissors, springs, files and goodness knows what else,
and besides these, music too. And how well! It's terrifying how much the people
here manage to achieve.' And Camille Saint-Saëns was quoted in a Paris
newspaper: 'I wish people who describe the English as unmusical could hear the
Birmingham singers. This wonderful choir has everything: intonation, perfect timing
and rhythm, finely shaded expression and a lovely sound; if people who sing like
this are not musical, well, they certainly perform as if they were the finest musicians
in the world.' It was a remarkable tribute from one of the leading composers of the
day to the Birmingham Festival Choral Society (established under that name in
1845 but whose history stretched back to the earliest festivals in the 1760s).

Under conductor-in-chief Hans Richter, over the next 24 years the festivals
reached their highest point with the successive introduction of Elgar's major choral
works, beginning in 1900 with *The Dream of Gerontius*. It summed up an
immensely rich period: no wonder that the Oxford Companion to Music could
remark, when commenting on the encouragement that the British festivals in
general had given to the development of oratorio, 'Birmingham's record is
especially to be noted'.

Town Hall environs: note the position of the crenellated building in all four pictures.

ABOVE Site of the Town Hall, 1822.

RIGHT Congreve Street. The buildings on the right were demolished to make way for the Council House in the 1870s.

LEFT View across to
Paradise Street.

BELOW Sketch
showing the portico
of Christ Church
(right) at the top of
New Street.

RIGHT Artist's impression of the hall 'now erecting'. As well as being 'intended to celebrate Musical Festivals … The Hall for the purposes of Town's Meetings will contain upwards of 8000 (sic) persons'.

BELOW A view of the interior, c1845.

LEFT 1834: Official
picture of the first
Triennial Musical
Festival to be held in
the Town Hall.

BELOW Birmingham
Musical Festival –
'arrival of the
company at the
Town Hall'.

RIGHT
1858: Elaborate
preparations for
Queen Victoria's visit.

BELOW
Queen Victoria
listens to an address
of welcome.

ABOVE
1854: Inaugural
dinner of the
Corporation of
Birmingham.

LEFT
1855: A banquet for
Prince Albert, Queen
Victoria's Consort.

ABOVE
1863: The Town
Hall illuminated for
the marriage of
Albert Edward,
Prince of Wales, to
Alexandra, daughter
of the King of
Denmark.

RIGHT Soireé of the
members of the
British Association.

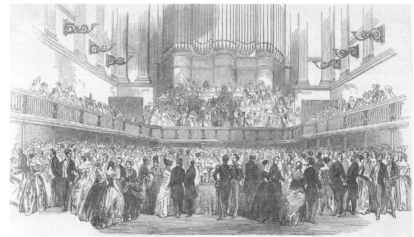

REPORT OF THE PROCEEDINGS

OF THE GREAT

ANTI-SLAVERY MEETING,

HELD AT THE

Town Hall, Birmingham,

ON WEDNESDAY, OCTOBER 14th, 1835;

WITH

AN APPENDIX,

CONTAINING

NOTICES OF THE CONDITION

OF

THE APPRENTICED LABOURERS

IN THE

WEST INDIES,

UNDER

THE ACT FOR THE ABOLITION OF SLAVERY

IN

THE BRITISH COLONIES.

"I have seen what has been done by the West Indian Assemblies. It is arrant trifling. They have done little, and what they have done is good for nothing; for it is totally destitute of an executory principle. This is the point to which I have applied my whole diligence. It is easy enough to say what shall be done:—to cause it to be done, hic labor, hoc opus"
Letter to the Right Hon. Henry Dundas (afterwards Viscount Melville), from the Right Hon. Edmund Burke, in the year 1792.

BIRMINGHAM:
PRINTED BY B. HUDSON, 18, BULL STREET.
1835.

Price Three-pence.

THE

REPORT

OF THE

BIRMINGHAM

ANTI-SLAVERY COMMITTEE,

PRESENTED AT THE ANNUAL MEETING,

HELD IN THE TOWN-HALL, BIRMINGHAM, AUGUST 1, 1838;

AND ALSO THE

PROCEEDINGS AT BIRMINGHAM,

ON

THE 1ST AND 2ND OF AUGUST,

IN

COMMEMORATION OF THE ABOLITION OF NEGRO APPREN-
TICESHIP IN THE BRITISH COLONIES,

As Reported expressly for the " Sun" Newspaper, with Corrections.

PRINTED FOR THE COMMITTEE
OF THE
BIRMINGHAM ANTI-SLAVERY SOCIETY.

1838.

Charles Dickens in action: he was keen that his reading of *A Christmas Carol* should be open to 'work-people'.

RIGHT 1833:
The appeal launched
to build the Town
Hall organ.

FAR RIGHT
Final position of the
organ, moved back
at Mendelssohn's
suggestion into a
newly-created area.

GRAND ORGAN,
INTENDED TO BE ERECTED IN THE NEW HALL, AT BIRMINGHAM,
FOR THE USE OF THE MUSICAL FESTIVALS.

THE ORGAN CASE will be Forty feet wide, and Forty-five feet high.

The largest metal diapason pipe, which is seen in the centre of the front of the Organ, will be Five feet three inches in circumference, and Thirty-five feet in height.

The largest wood diapason pipe will be of such large dimensions that the interior will measure upwards of 200 cubic feet.

In the full Organ will be Ten open diapasons, and all the other parts will be in proportion to it.

There will be Sixty draw stops, and Five sets of keys.

To supply this stupendous instrument with wind will require many bellows, the whole superficial measure of which will exceed 380 feet; and to give, if possible, some further idea of its magnitude, it may be mentioned that its weight is estimated altogether at upwards of Forty tons.

This magnificent Organ will thus have much greater power than any on the Continent; and it may be observed, that the extensive Hall in which it is to be erected, is one of the largest and best proportioned rooms in Europe, without a column or impediment to obstruct the proper vibration of the sound, and is thus fully equal to display the full grandeur of the Instrument.

An Organ upon this grand and extended scale cannot be procured under a very heavy cost; and as no funds have been appropriated towards its purchase by the Act of Parliament under which the Hall is erected, it becomes necessary, in order to enable the Committee to accomplish their object, that a sum of not less than £2,000 should be raised by voluntary contributions, in addition to any other means the Committee may possess.

When, however, it is considered that such an Organ is indispensably requisite for the production of those great Choral effects which have rendered the Birmingham Festivals so attractive, and that from these Festivals the General Hospital has derived a large portion of its annual income for many years, the Festival Committee appeal with confidence to the public spirit and liberality, and cannot permit themselves to doubt that the Nobility and Gentry who have heretofore patronised the Festivals, as well as the Inhabitants of Birmingham and its vicinity, will come forward with their aid towards the Subscription for erecting this Organ.

They venture likewise to hope that all the admirers and patrons of Sacred and Choral Music, which has been brought to such perfection in this country, will lend their assistance on the occasion—and thus contribute to the support of the Birmingham Musical Festivals, on a scale commensurate with the high character they have so long maintained, and the benevolent object for which they were established, and have been hitherto successfully continued.

Subscriptions will be received at the Bank of Messrs. TAYLORS and LLOYDS, in Birmingham (Treasurers to the General Hospital), and at Messrs. HANBURYS, TAYLOR, and Co's, 60, Lombard-street, London.

THE GRAND ORGAN IN THE TOWN HALL BIRMINGHAM.

RIGHT
The assembled
audience and title
page of *Elijah*,
premièred at the
Town Hall
in 1846.

BELOW
A pencil sketch of
Mendelssohn
in 1842

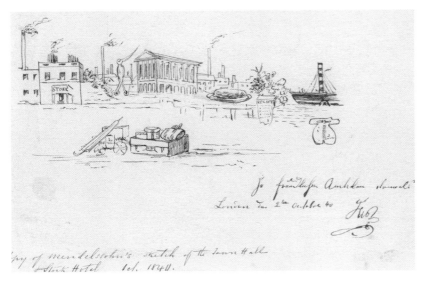

Mendelssohn's own impressions of Birmingham, 1840.

The Birmingham Festival commissioned new works from leading composers of the day who came to conduct them.
Clockwise: Camille Saint-Saëns, Edvard Grieg, Charles Gounod and Arthur Sullivan.

LEFT One of the concert programmes from the 1867 Festival.

BELOW Photomontage of artists and composers at the same Festival.

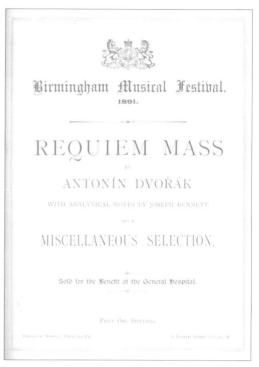

ABOVE AND RIGHT
Dvořák's Requiem Mass (1891)
was one of the Festivals' most
important commissions.

BELOW Concert-goers leaving
the 1888 Triennial Festival.

Birmingham Sunday School Union.

PROGRAMME

OF THE

Annual ✧ Scholars' ✧ Festival

TO BE HELD ON

MONDAY, TUESDAY, WEDNESDAY & THURSDAY,

September 27th, 28th, 29th, and 30th, 1880,

IN THE TOWN HALL, BIRMINGHAM.

SUBJECT :—

Songs ✧ of ✧ Many ✧ Lands

ILLUSTRATED BY A

Beautiful Series of Dissolving Views.

The Descriptive Lecture will be given by the Rev. ARTHUR MURSELL.

THE MUSICAL PORTION OF THE FESTIVAL WILL BE RENDERED BY A

CHOIR ✧ OF ✧ ABOVE ✧ FIVE ✧ HUNDRED ✧ VOICES,

UNDER THE DIRECTION OF

A. R. GAUL, ESQ.,

(Mus. Bac., Cantab,)

ACCOMPANIED BY AN EFFICIENT MILITARY BAND.

THE CHAIR WILL BE TAKEN EACH EVENING AT HALF-PAST SIX O'CLOCK.

ADMISSION :

Junior Scholars, Twopence ; Teachers and Senior Scholars, Fourpence ; Friends, Side Galleries,
and Front of Great Gallery, One Shilling each.

PUBLISHED BY THE BIRMINGHAM SUNDAY SCHOOL UNION.
1880.

Entered at Stationers' Hall.

PRINTED BY T. H. LAKINS, EDMUND STREET, BIRMINGHAM.

RIGHT The famous Lloyd George riot in 1901.

BELOW Twenty years later all seems to have been forgiven.

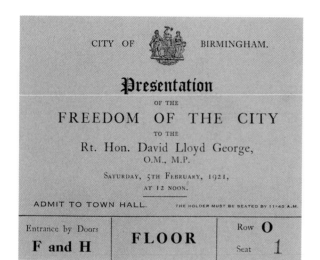

THE RIOT AT BIRMINGHAM TOWN HALL
(From a Sketch by Allan Stewart.)

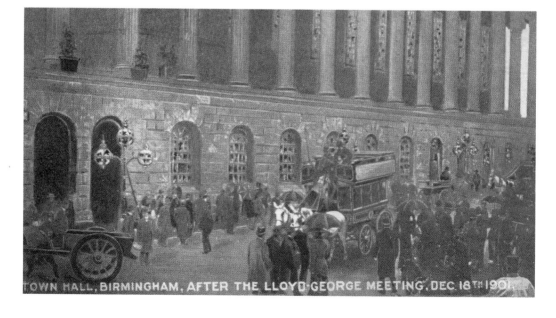

TOWN HALL, BIRMINGHAM, AFTER THE LLOYD-GEORGE MEETING. DEC 18TH 1901.

UNITED IRISH LEAGUE

St. Patrick's Day
CELEBRATION.

A Public Demonstration

WILL BE HELD AT

THE TOWN HALL, BIRMINGHAM,

ON THURSDAY, 16th MARCH, 1905.

Messrs. J. F. X. O'BRIEN, M.P. & J. P. HAYDEN, M.P.

Will deliver Addresses on the **Irish Political Situation.**

Chair to be taken by DR. HENNESSY, B.A., at 8 p.m., supported by all the prominent Irish Nationalists of the City.

"Bishop O'Donnell wishes the United Irish League Meeting on the 16th a hearty God's speed."

Grand Irish Concert

To follow, in which will take part :

MRS. MULLANY and Miss Showell, Miss Brooks, Miss Hurst and Little Madge;
Mr. J. D. Davies, Tenor; Mr. E. Magrath, Bass (both of the Brythoniaid Quartet ;
MR. TOM PHILBIN, as Soloists ; and the Brythoniaid (Welsh) Quartet.

Organ Recital at 7 p.m.   Doors open at 6.30 p.m.

Tickets to be only had at Entrance Doors E and J of the Town Hall.

Admission: Side Galleries and Front of Great Gallery, 1/-; Floor and Back of Great Gallery, 6d.

Banquet at 'Ye Olde Royal,' Temple Row,

ON TUESDAY, 14th MARCH, 1905, AT 8 P.M.

CHAIRMAN ... MR. JAMES O'DOHERTY.

TICKETS 3 - EACH, for which apply to Hon. Secs., Mr. Ml. Murtagh, 54 Ledsam Street;
Mr. T. O. Grogan, 27 Devonshire Street, Soho.

Ceuo mile ḟáilte ṗomaṫ !   GOD SAVE IRELAND !

O'Brien & Ards, Printers, Dublin.   Irish Paper.

1902: The Council House (BELOW) and Town Hall (RIGHT) illuminated to celebrate the coronation of King Edward VII.

The changing face of Birmingham: Paradise Street and the Town Hall with Christ Church in 1896 (ABOVE),
replaced by Galloways' Corner by 1905 (BELOW).

Town Hall, Birmingham.

ABOVE A turn-of-the-century postcard.

RIGHT The Rt Hon Joseph Chamberlain, his wife at his side, addresses a constituency rally.

CITIZENS' COMMITTEE

TO PROTEST AGAINST THE PROSECUTIONS UNDER THE

MUTINY ACT.

A PUBLIC DEMONSTRATION

will be held in the

BIRMINGHAM TOWN HALL,

ON

Friday, April 12th, at 8 p.m.

Speakers: JOSIAH WEDGEWOOD, M.P. and others

Come and Protest against the Arrest and Imprisonment
of Crowsley, Bowman, the brothers Buck, and Tom Mann,
for urging Soldiers not to shoot unarmed people.

Freedom of Speech is in Danger.

1912

ABOVE The Halford Orchestra in 1903. On conductor George Halford's right, violinist Fritz Kreisler.

RIGHT Title page of the autograph full score of Elgar's *The Dream of Gerontius*, a Festival commission of 1900, signed on the right by the soloists and conductor Hans Richter.

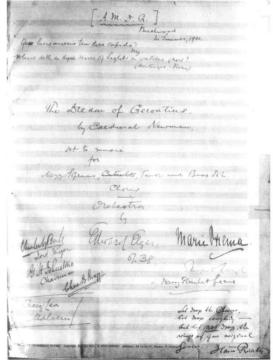

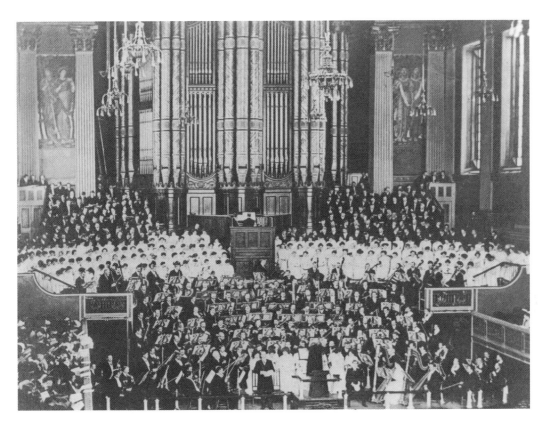

ABOVE 1909: Hans Richter conducts Elgar's *The Dream of Gerontius* at his last Festival. Note the wall murals by Edward Burne Jones on either side of the organ.

LEFT "Not arrested, but protected (against autograph vampires) …" wrote Hans Richter.

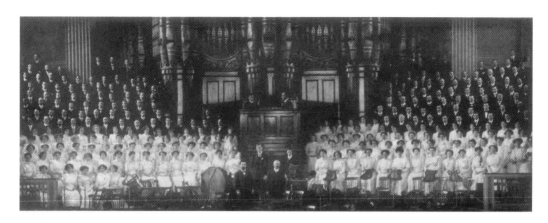

TOP 1912: The last of the
Birmingham Triennial Musical Festivals
included premières by Elgar and
Bantock besides the first UK
performance of Sibelius's Fourth
Symphony. Sir Henry Wood (bearded)
was the Festival conductor.

ABOVE Jean Sibelius.

RIGHT Edward Elgar with
Granville Bantock.

CHAPTER TWO

1913 – 1939

The 1927 reconstruction

THE FIRST
RECONSTRUCTION

SOCIALLY THE YEARS BETWEEN THE TWO WORLD WARS saw significant change and much deprivation. It was a period that found the Town Hall in use at various times as an armed forces recruitment centre, for issuing ration books, and later to distribute food to children of the poor during the recession. Charity fayres for the benefit of Dr Barnardo's Homes and bazaars in aid of the 'Waifs and Strays' were typical of the time. Patriotic meetings, to which Birmingham people were urged to 'come in your thousands', tumbled over one another: subjects such as 'The Upholding of British Honour', 'Christianity and the World Crisis' and the Anglo-Catholic Congress filled the building. Musically, the Hall was still predominantly a classical venue, though the Triennial Festivals were not revived after 1912 and so the customary procession of famous composers, singers and instrumentalists largely petered out. For the moment most music was provided by local concerts, the occasional visiting orchestra or opera performance (in the Prince of Wales Theatre where Symphony Hall now stands).

Out of a period of hesitancy grew the desire for something that Birmingham had never had: a permanent orchestra bearing the city's name. This came about in 1920 when the City of Birmingham Orchestra (CBO) was established with municipal support. Elgar conducted its first Town Hall concert, Adrian Boult became permanent conductor within a few years, and the orchestra settled down in what was to be its home for the next seven decades. There was a setback in 1925 when part of the

roof collapsed, triggering the decision to make significant changes to the 90-year old interior, notably by remodelling the shape of the existing gallery and adding a completely new one above it. This established seating at 2,000, but adversely affected the acoustics by creating patches of 'dead' sound at the rear of the Hall, while the platform was at first dissected by the newly-designed gallery's balustrades which marched uninterrupted across it; they had subsequently to be made removable so that an orchestra could sit in its accustomed format.

The Hall reopened in April 1927 with a grand concert that sought to recapture some of the glamour of earlier times and, throughout the 1930s, the CBO added to its laurels, under Leslie Heward's conductorship (1930–43) showing itself to be fully conversant with both the standard repertoire and the new music of the day. By the time the Hall celebrated its centenary in 1934 Birmingham could be seen once more to be an important centre for music, its international reputation boosted when world-famous solo artists such as the pianist Vladimir Horowitz and great orchestras such as the Berlin and Vienna Philharmonics arrived; the composer Rachmaninov gave a rare piano recital and 22-year old violinist Yehudi Menuhin chose Birmingham to begin a ten-concert tour of Britain. Meanwhile the CBO itself was capable of attracting eminent international soloists such as Artur Schnabel, Adolf Busch and Edwin Fischer together with guest conductors of the highest calibre. One of these was the celebrated Austro-German Felix Weingartner, whose concert attracted an audience in excess of the building's capacity (by 50: where the extra people were somehow accommodated is not recorded). Weingartner was quite overcome when told that Mendelssohn had conducted in the Town Hall, and was to be seen walking about, touching the walls reverently, and declaring: "Ziss vass holy groundt."

In 1937, for the joyful celebrations surrounding the coronation of King George VI, the Hall's exterior columns were garlanded and decorated with the arms of the Lords of the Manor of Birmingham since 1166. Two years later the mood was very different. Neville Chamberlain, the former city councillor, Lord Mayor and MP for Ladywood, who had followed in his father Joseph's footsteps, now found himself thrust into the spotlight as the nation's Prime Minister. After war was declared in September 1939 he travelled the UK reporting on its progress and rallying the people, and found no warmer welcome than in Birmingham when he spoke in the Town Hall. Not long before, it had been used as an army recruitment centre and was now sand-bagged against the threat of enemy action. At Chamberlain's side, as First Lord of the Admiralty, stood Winston Churchill, already a familiar figure in the city where he had first spoken on the same platform in 1928. The Prime Minister's message was unequivocal: "The war must be won. Until we are satisfied that freedom is safe, we will continue to do battle with all our soul and with all our strength."

ABOVE
1914: Men queue
outside the Town
Hall to enlist for War.
The building was
adapted as a
recruiting office
(RIGHT).

ABOVE 1917: Prime Minister Lloyd George launched a nationwide public appeal to 'lend and save', for the war effort, through the Tank Bank.

LEFT 1916: The famous suffragette, Mrs Emmeline Pankhurst, toured Britain encouraging enlistment.

ABOVE 1920: The City of
Birmingham Orchestra (CBO)
with founder conductor
Appleby Matthews

RIGHT Adrian Boult, CBO
conductor 1924–30

SOME CBO GUEST
CONDUCTORS 1920–39

ABOVE, LEFT TO RIGHT
Eugene Goossens; Malcolm
Sargent; Bruno Walter.

LEFT International musicians
included the composer
Maurice Ravel

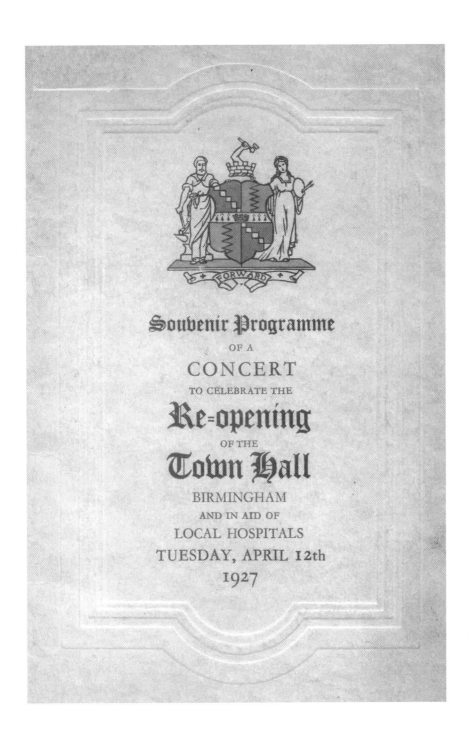

Souvenir Programme

OF A

CONCERT

TO CELEBRATE THE

Re=opening

OF THE

Town Hall

BIRMINGHAM

AND IN AID OF

LOCAL HOSPITALS

TUESDAY, APRIL 12th

1927

The Great Gallery
before (RIGHT) and
after (BELOW)
reconstruction
1925–7.

1927: The new Gallery's balustrades can be seen to divide the concert platform in two.

RIGHT An early example of sponsorship – somewhat mismatched perhaps.

BELOW 'Street Lighting and "Relief" Illumination in Birmingham – A Fine Example', according to the Gas Journal, 1931.

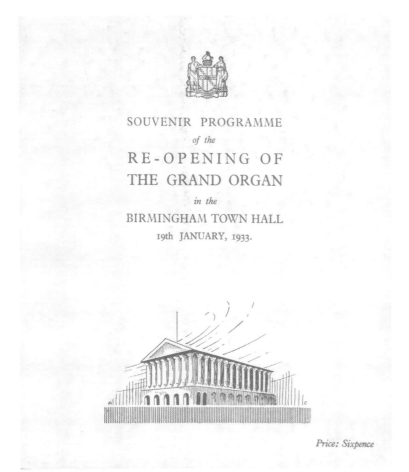

SOUVENIR PROGRAMME
of the
RE-OPENING OF
THE GRAND ORGAN
in the
BIRMINGHAM TOWN HALL
19th JANUARY, 1933.

Price: Sixpence

THE FIRST BIRMINGHAM
CITY ORGANISTS

FROM LEFT
James Stimpson (1842–86),
C W Perkins (1888–1923),
George Cunningham
(1924–49).

RIGHT Felix
Weingartner's
1938 CBO concert
is reported to
have drawn an
audience of 2050.

BELOW
Leslie Heward,
CBO conductor
1930–43.

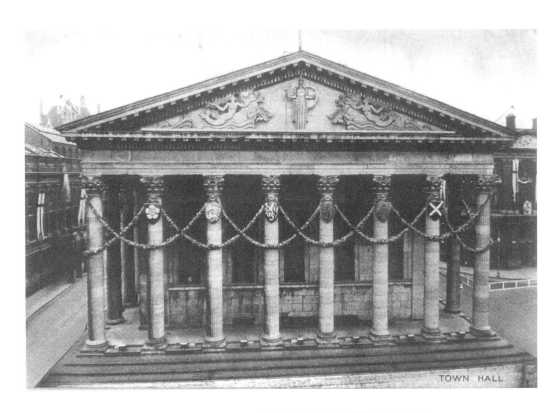

ABOVE
1937: The Town Hall decorated for the coronation of King George VI.

LEFT
1939: Command performance. King George VI and Queen Elizabeth watching a display entitled 'A Pageant of Fitness'.

Birmingham's claim to have more canals than Venice goes back a long way as these two light-hearted postcards show.

CHAPTER THREE
1940–1959

Preparing for war: sand bags and water tanks in Victoria Square

CHANGE OF TUNE

SOME OF THE MORE UNUSUAL USES to which the Town Hall was put both during the war and in its aftermath feature on the pages that follow. International Women's Day was celebrated in 1946, and later the same year Mrs Attlee, wife of the Prime Minister, was guest of honour at a Women's Victory Rally. In 1943 there had been an international conference to discuss 'Science under Fascism and Democracy' and, in 1947, came an exhibition to explain the Allies' plans to restore government in Germany. Musically, the gap created by the non-appearance of foreign artists was filled by British orchestras such as the Hallé and Liverpool Philharmonic with their conductors John Barbirolli and Malcolm Sargent; one of the very few international artists to return was Yehudi Menuhin, whose concert was in aid of the Belgian Red Cross.

Just a year after the declaration of war in September 1939 the first air-raids on Birmingham took the Town Hall intermittently out of use. The CBO struggled on, even managing to make its first recordings there, but it must have been an uncomfortable experience in a snowy December with no heating and many of the windows blown out. Soprano Gwen Catley retained her fur coat and rubber boots while singing some songs into the microphone, and the players had to peg their music to the music-stands to stop it blowing away. Before each song the gramophone men deployed a hooter on the roof to scare away Birmingham's prodigious starling population, whose noise would otherwise find its way onto the discs; blasts of the hooter gave five minutes respite and allowed each 78rpm side to be completed – before the birds came swarming back, and the process had to begin again. These adverse conditions forced the Orchestra to migrate to other Midlands halls; making records in Dudley they were joined by the celebrated Birmingham-born singer Webster Booth, who was perhaps disappointed to be denied the chance of recording in the city of his birth.

Upon Leslie Heward's death in 1943 George Weldon proved a popular replacement, placing the orchestra on a permanent basis, in 1948 putting the 'S' (for 'symphony') into CBO and introducing promenade concerts. The public appetite for music was greater than ever, and the players worked extremely hard, frequently repeating items to meet the insistent demand; when a critic observed mildly that the CBSO 'must know *Greensleeves* backwards by now' a wit in the orchestra wrote it out backwards and the orchestra played it. Weldon was followed in 1951 by Rudolf Schwarz, Andrzej Panufnik took over in 1957, and artistically it was a good period, with distinguished conductors including Sir Thomas Beecham, Pierre Monteux and Jascha Horenstein guest-conducting the CBSO and the big names of the time such as singers Elisabeth Schumann and Beniamino Gigli and the pianists Alfred Cortot and Artur Rubinstein all coming to the Town Hall platform. The Berlin Philharmonic reappeared, the Philadelphia Orchestra began its first-ever European tour in Birmingham (1949), and the Amsterdam Concertgebouw and Israel Philharmonic also paid first visits, though the Dutch conductor Eduard van Beinum sent a review of his Town Hall concert to a composer whose music had figured in the programme with the cryptic comment: 'Enclosed a criticism. *Rubbish.'*

A newer musical manifestation that appeared in the post-war years saw the old building 'rocking' in a way not witnessed before. Newer styles of singing imported from the USA (typified by Elvis Presley with what were termed his 'pelvic gyrations', and on record by Johnnie Ray, Rosemary Clooney and others) were soon taken up by British songwriters, and an emerging breed of British singers – Cliff Richard, Alma Cogan and Shirley Bassey among them – began to appear in concert as well as on records and the radio. Before the end of the 1950s Tommy Steele and Lonnie Donegan were skiffling merrily away, and Birmingham welcomed Buddy Holly and the Crickets, one of the first US groups to bring rock & roll to the UK. Another new development saw all-night jazz sessions in the Town Hall with names such as Acker Bilk and Terry Lightfoot on the bill. Meanwhile, 'trad jazz' had a distinct hard-core following that was determined to resist change. In jazz circles it was understood that, if Birmingham liked you, the applause could go for five minutes but, if not, the audience would throw corporation toilet rolls and pennies. At one of the more bizarre incidents in 1953 when band-leader Humphrey Lyttelton decided to introduce an alto saxophone into his band's line-up, each time the unfortunate player stepped forward for a solo 'spot' not only was it received in stony silence but a whole row of Town Hall die-hards solemnly raised a banner bearing the words GO-HOME-DIRTY-BOPPER …

Prime Minister Neville Chamberlain
speaks about the war in 1940.
On his left, partly hidden, is
Winston Churchill.

Sand bagging the windows after the announcement of hostilities.

YOU ARE INVITED

TO AN

INTERNATIONAL CONFERENCE

ON

SCIENCE under FASCISM and DEMOCRACY

IN THE

TOWN HALL, BIRMINGHAM

SUNDAY, AUGUST 22, at 3-0

1943

THE LORD MAYOR WILL WELCOME THE DELEGATES

Speakers :

J. B. S. HALDANE, F.R.S.	BRITAIN
S. H. HILDEBRAND	U.S.A.
P. M. YAP	CHINA
M. FOURNIER	FRANCE
A. V. ANROOY, F.R.S.	HOLLAND
D. SCHOBER	CZECHOSLOVAKIA
A. FISCHER	AUSTRIA
J. G. SIEBERT	GERMANY

Professor M. L. E. OLIPHANT, F.R.S., Chairman

ADMISSION TO CONFERENCE FREE

FOLLOWED BY AN

INTERNATIONAL FILM SHOW

IN THE TOWN HALL, 7-0 p.m. to 9-0 p.m.

Admission 1/-   Tickets obtained at doors

Note.—Limited refreshments will be available for those attending both Conference and Film Show

ORGANISED by the ASSOCIATION of SCIENTIFIC WORKERS

Revival ! Healing ! Prophecy !

THE TOWN HALL,

BIRMINGHAM.

AUGUST BANK HOLIDAY MONDAY

(August 2nd) 1943

at **3 and 6.30** p.m.

Preacher :

PRINCIPAL GEORGE JEFFREYS

(The Famous Revivalist)

with his **REVIVAL PARTY**

Soloist :

JOAN McWHIRTER

Those seeking bodily healing will be prayed for according to the Scriptures.

All Seats Free !   Do not miss these Two Special Meetings !

Crystal Publications, Ltd., Upper Norwood. S.E.19.

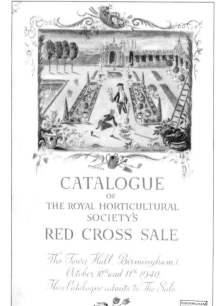

CATALOGUE

OF

THE ROYAL HORTICULTURAL SOCIETY'S

RED CROSS SALE

The Town Hall, Birmingham 1.
October 10th and 11th 1940
This Catalogue admits to The Sale

GERMANY
under control
(The Second Phase)

A selection of wartime posters

INTERNATIONAL WOMEN'S DAY
TOWN HALL CELEBRATIONS

To Unite All Women irrespective of Race, Politics, Creed

As	For
Wives	Peace
Mothers	Equality
Workers	Security
Citizens	Opportunity

Friday, March 15, 1946
7.30 p.m.
TOWN HALL   BIRMINGHAM

Chairman   -   The Lady Mayoress

Speakers - Mrs. Mavis Tate (Late M.P. for Frome)   Greetings from International Visitors
Mrs. Barbara Lewis (Parliamentary Candidate for Wandsworth, 1945)
Choir conducted by Prof. J. A. WESTRUP, M.A., D.Mus. (Oxon), F.R.C.O., (Professor of Music Birmingham University)

Doors Open 7 p.m.   -   -   Organ Recital from 7.0 to 7.30 p.m.

Orchestra and Upper Gallery FREE
Floor and Lower Gallery 1/- Seats Reserved until 7.30 p.m.

Tickets from Alan Priestley, 27b Paradise Street, Birmingham

WOMEN'S SACRIFICE MUST NOT BE IN VAIN

Olton Printing Company, 1231 Warwick Road, Birmingham 27

CITY OF BIRMINGHAM
MUNICIPAL OFFICERS' GUILD

**Welcome Home Concert
to Members returned
✦ from service with His ✦
Majesty's Forces during
the World War**
1939–1945

TOWN HALL
WEDNESDAY, 27TH MARCH
1946

Yehudi Menuhin was always one of the most welcome
international performers, appearing at the Town Hall over
five decades from 1938. The programme dates from 1943.

Town Hall · Birmingham
Sunday, March 28th, at 6·15 p.m.
(by arrangement with Harold Holt, Ltd.)

Concert

Recital by
YEHUDI MENUHIN
with
MARCEL GAZELLE
at the Piano

In aid of the
BELGIAN RED CROSS
(UNDER THE AUSPICES OF THE
BELGIAN GOVERNMENT)

Programme
Price 6d.

Wartime City of Birmingham Orchestra (CBO) with conductor George Weldon (1943–51) in concert and at rehearsal.

ABOVE
CBO Promenaders: with the Stalls seating removed, paper sheets were provided for people to sit on the floor.

LEFT Sitting- as well as standing-room only at the Last Night of the Proms.

Wilhelm Furtwängler arrives in Birmingham for his concert.

TOWN HALL, BIRMINGHAM.

Friday, November 5th, 1948, at 7 p.m.

BERLIN PHILHARMONIC ORCHESTRA
(Leader: SIEGFRIED BORRIES)

CHARITY CONCERT SPONSORED BY
CHRISTIAN ACTION

Patrons:
THE EARL OF HALIFAX   SIR STAFFORD CRIPPS
Chairman: The REV. CANON L. JOHN COLLINS

Concerts Committee:
The REV. CANON L. JOHN COLLINS (Chairman), LADY CRIPPS, D.B.E., WALTER GREENWOOD,
HOWARD MARSHALL, E. G. D. LIVEING (Hon. Secretary)

Proceeds in aid of the International Work of CHRISTIAN ACTION for promoting
Friendship and Understanding in Europe

Conductor:
DR. WILHELM

FURTWÄNGLER

PROGRAMME
SIXPENCE

Management:
IBBS & TILLETT, Ltd.
124, Wigmore Street, W.1

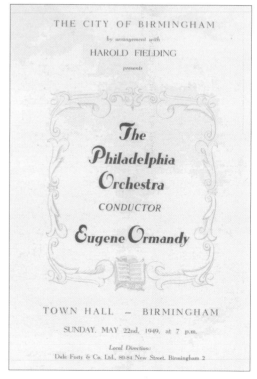

THE CITY OF BIRMINGHAM
by arrangement with
HAROLD FIELDING
presents

The
Philadelphia
Orchestra
CONDUCTOR
Eugene Ormandy

TOWN HALL — BIRMINGHAM
SUNDAY, MAY 22nd, 1949, at 7 p.m.

Local Direction:
Dale Forty & Co. Ltd., 80-84 New Street, Birmingham 2

SOME INTERNATIONAL CONDUCTORS
CLOCKWISE FROM TOP LEFT Eduard van Beinum, Pierre Monteux, Alceo Galliera and Jascha Horenstein.

Always a full house for Sir Thomas: Beecham and the CBO in 1954.

A PLETHORA OF PIANISTS

CLOCKWISE Moura Lympany,
Solomon, Dame Myra Hess and
Clifford Curzon

OPPOSITE PAGE Denis Matthews
and Eileen Joyce.

BIRMINGHAM PIANOFORTE SUBSCRIPTION CONCERTS

SEASON 1950-51

Directed by IBBS & TILLETT LTD., 124 Wigmore Street, London, W.1

TOWN HALL
BIRMINGHAM

MONDAY EVENINGS at 7.0

OCTOBER 23, 1950   FEBRUARY 5, 1951
NOVEMBER 13, 1950   MARCH 5, 1951

SUBSCRIPTION FOR **24/-, 20/- 16/-** INCLUDING
FOUR CONCERTS   **14/- & 10/-**   TAX

Concert Direction and Box Office:
ALAN G. PRIESTLEY, LTD.
27½ Paradise Street, Birmingham, I
(Telephone: MIDland 0021-0134)

Box Office Open Daily 9 a.m. to 6 p.m.

MASTER WORKS OF PIANO MUSIC OF
THE 19th CENTURY PLAYED BY WORLD
FAMOUS ARTISTS

C O R T O T
MOISEIWITSCH
EDWIN FISCHER
IRENE SCHARRER

Australian soprano Joan Hammond achieved early fame through the records she made with the CBO at the Town Hall.

THE TOWN HALL
BIRMINGHAM

TUESDAY, 22nd JANUARY, 1952
at 7 p.m.

The English Opera Group

presents

KATHLEEN FERRIER
(Contralto)

PETER PEARS
(Tenor)

BENJAMIN BRITTEN
(Piano)

Arias by Purcell, Handel, Arne and Gluck
Lieder by Schubert
Folksongs
A new Canticle, especially composed by Benjamin Britten

TICKETS:
Lower Gallery 7/6, 6/-   Upper Gallery 6/-, 5/-, 4/-
Ground Floor 5/-, 3/-   Orchestra 3/-

From Alan G. Priestley, Ltd., 27b Paradise Street, Birmingham.
(MIDland 0021)

Gigli, the great
Italian tenor.

JACK HYLTON and HAROLD FIELDING announce

BENIAMINO GIGLI RECITAL TOUR

SPRING 1952

MONDAY	FEBRUARY	25TH	ROYAL ALBERT HALL (Manager: C. S. Taylor)	LONDON	7.30
THURSDAY	FEBRUARY	28TH	CITY HALL (A Sheffield Philharmonic Society Concert)	SHEFFIELD	7.00
TUESDAY	MARCH	4TH	ST. ANDREW'S HALL	GLASGOW	7.30
SUNDAY	MARCH	9TH	CITY HALL	NEWCASTLE	3.00
THURSDAY	MARCH	13TH	ROYAL ALBERT HALL (Manager: C. S. Taylor)	LONDON	7.30
SUNDAY	MARCH	16TH	FLORAL HALL (A Corporation of Scarborough Concert)	SCARBOROUGH	3.15
WEDNESDAY	MARCH	19TH	TOWN HALL	BIRMINGHAM	7.00
MONDAY	MARCH	24TH	BELLE VUE (A Hallé Concerts Society Concert)	MANCHESTER	7.00
THURSDAY	MARCH	27TH	SOPHIA GARDENS PAVILION (A City of Cardiff Concert)	CARDIFF	7.30
WEDNESDAY	APRIL	2ND	CIVIC HALL (A Corporation of Wolverhampton Concert)	WOLVERHAMPTON	7.00
SUNDAY	APRIL	20TH	COLSTON HALL (A Corporation of Bristol Concert)	BRISTOL	7.00
WEDNESDAY	APRIL	23RD	KING GEORGE'S HALL (A Blackburn Music Society Concert)	BLACKBURN	7.30
WEDNESDAY	APRIL	30TH	DE MONTFORT HALL (A Corporation of Leicester Concert)	LEICESTER	7.00

Details regarding the above concerts can be obtained from:
HAROLD FIELDING : FIELDING HOUSE : HAYMARKET : S.W.1 (Whitehall 4045)

1948: King George VI, with Queen Elizabeth, speaking at the Town Hall (BELOW). 300,000 people turned out to welcome them.

THE BRITISH-SOVIET SOCIETY

(Birmingham Branch)

PRESENTS

PAUL ROBESON

AT THE

Birmingham Town Hall

ON

Saturday, May 21st, 1949

at 7·0 p.m.

PAUL ROBESON, son of a run-away slave, who became a minister of the Church, became himself a tower of learning and sport at College and Havard University. He practised law before his voice and acting ability gave him a pre-eminent place.

Paul is 51, and the working class movement greet him as one who remains the unspoilt, lovable person known to millions for his contributions to Art and Human Progress.

He made his first success before he left law school, in "Emperor Jones". In England in 1922 acted with Mrs. Pat Campbell.   In 1928 made his first great popular success in "Show Boat".   From then he has been world famous.

Gradually he began to see that although he was doing alright, ten million of his fellow negros in the American South lived on the edge of starvation.   He says of his first visit to the Soviet Union, "It was like stepping into another planet." I felt the full dignity of being a human being for the first time.   He loved what he found there so much, that he returned to Russia each year and also sent his son to school there.

Programme - Price 6d

1949: Paul Robeson appeared twice at the Town Hall, as both singer and civil rights campaigner.

ABOVE   Hardly an un-hatted head: Women's rally, 1950.

RIGHT   Prime Minister Attlee receives the freedom of the City.

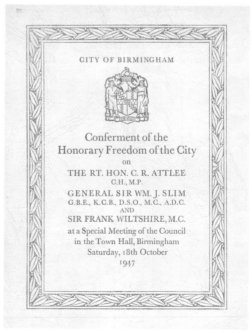

CITY OF BIRMINGHAM

Conferment of the
Honorary Freedom of the City
on
THE RT. HON. C. R. ATTLEE
C.H., M.P.
GENERAL SIR WM. J. SLIM
G.B.E., K.C.B., D.S.O., M.C., A.D.C.
AND
SIR FRANK WILTSHIRE, M.C.
at a Special Meeting of the Council
in the Town Hall, Birmingham
Saturday, 18th October
1947

LEFT 1958: Oswald Mosley, Leader of the extreme right-wing British Union movement.

BELOW 1962: His rallies frequently resulted in scuffles. Birmingham was no exception.

RIGHT 1954: Benjamin
Britten at the premiere
of his *Gloriana* Suite.
Rudolf Schwarz
conducted the CBSO.

BELOW Birmingham
premiere: pianist Louis
Kentner (left) and CBSO
conductor Rudolf
Schwarz discuss
Michael Tippett's Piano
Concerto with the
composer (seated)
in 1956.

ABOVE In 1957 the Town Hall was an island site.

LEFT Decorated for a visit to Birmingham by Queen Elizabeth II in 1955.

1957: A 21" Town Hall sculpted in chocolate by Cadbury for a 'guess the weight' competition.

ABOVE The ebullient Dizzy Gillespie in his dressing room.

RIGHT Change of tune: a new musical era dawns.

JAZZ GREATS:

RIGHT
Humphrey Lyttelton
practising backstage.

BELOW
Duke Ellington.

LEFT Sidney Bechet in his dressing room.

BELOW Count Basie greets his fans.

RIGHT All-night jazz in
1959, 10.30pm–7am.

ABOVE Blues singer
Diane Day & George
Huxley's New Orleans
jazzmen at an all-night
jazz band ball.

JAZZSHOWS present

CARNIVAL OF JAZZ

LISTENING & DANCING TO

FRIDAY, OCTOBER 9th
10-30 p.m. - 7-0 a.m.

Compered by
George
Webb

Micky
Ashman
and his Jazz Band

Mr.
ACKER
BILK'S
Paramount Jazz
Band

Light
Refresh-
ments
Available

Terry
Lightfoot's
New Orleans Jazzmen

The
Second
City
Jazzmen

Accommodation is
strictly limited so
BOOK EARLY TO AVOID
DISAPPOINTMENT

Tickets 15s. each
from: BIRMINGHAM TOWN HALL
(Tel. CEN 1060)

BIRMINGHAM TOWN HALL

LEFT Rock and Roll from
the Town Hall in 1956.

BELOW Riding high:
Bill Haley's Comets.

RIGHT
1958: Buddy Holly
brought rock and
roll to Birmingham.

BELOW
A young Shirley
Bassey greets her
fans.

CHAPTER FOUR

1960–1979

MIDLAND TOP TEN

PRESENTS

THE ROLLING STONES

THE MARAUDERS
(LUCILLE)

DUKE D'MOND
and the
BARRON KNIGHTS
(PEANUT BUTTER)

Wayne Fontana and the Mindbenders
(LITTLE DARLIN')

PLUS LOCAL SUPPORTING GROUP

H.M.V. Recording Artistes **Denny Laine and the Diplomats**

AT THE

Town Hall, Birmingham
Wednesday, March 25th 1964
6.30. AND 8.45

TICKETS 4/6; 6/6; 8/6; 10/6 available

as from 7th March at the Town Hall Ticket Office and Agents.
Persons wishing to produce this leaflet at the Town Hall Booking
Office will be entitled to purchase tickets as from the 22nd February

Supporting group Denny Laine and the Diplomats included
Bev Bevan, later of ELO

PALACE
OF VARIETIES

THE BICENTENARY OF THE BIRMINGHAM TRIENNIAL FESTIVALS (taking the original founding date as 1768) was the occasion of their brief revival in 1968 and again in 1971, but they were not re-established. Some outstanding figures including the violinist Isaac Stern were attracted and Sir Adrian Boult returned to conduct *The Dream of Gerontius,* which had tended to supplant *Elijah* as Birmingham's most celebrated musical commission. *Elijah* still put in an occasional appearance, though when Dvořák's *Requiem* was revived in 1973 it was thought to be for the first time since the composer himself had conducted the 1891 première in Birmingham. From the beginning of the 1960s the CBSO's conductor for eight artistically fruitful years was Hugo Rignold, but when he resigned and was succeeded in 1969 by Louis Frémaux audience figures rose sharply to 83% and recording, not attempted in the Town Hall since the 1940s, was revived. Buoyed up by these developments the prospect of a new concert hall for Birmingham came into view, but financially the time was not right and the Town Hall soldiered on with occasional cosmetic attention such as the installation of double-glazing; and the platform, much altered over the years, saw yet another change with access to it being provided by a double stairway placed between it and the audience.

Aside from the CBSO the variety of musical fare on offer from visitors was as prodigious as ever. An influx of Russian musicians brought the legendary violinist David Oistrakh, the cellist Mstislav Rostropovich and the composer Shostakovich's son Maxim, while another famous family of musicians – the Torteliers, led by *père* Paul – became regular visitors. Birmingham heard the early joint recitals of guitarists Julian Bream and John Williams, while new to the scene was the valuable series of concerts (eventually 38) sponsored by the philanthropic Birmingham shop-owner Reginald Vincent that introduced singers including Elisabeth Schwarzkopf and Victoria de los Angeles and great pianists such as Wilhelm Kempff to the city. One otherwise unremarkable date in the summer of 1976 saw the Merseyside Youth Orchestra arrive for a single concert with a dynamic young 19-year old conductor: his name was Simon Rattle … The equally youthful cellist Jacqueline du Pré gave a recital with her husband-to-be,

Daniel Barenboim. Lighter fare was provided by the Danish comedian Victor Borge, Mantovani and his Orchestra came, and the Town Hall displayed an unexpected versatility by staging a full-dress performance of Gilbert & Sullivan's *The Mikado* – not to mention the World Power Lifting Championships.

Elsewhere much was happening in other areas of music. The Town Hall's staid interior had already surrendered to all-night 'Rock n'Twist' sessions, and it was only a short time before the phenomenon known as The Beatles leapt into the limelight, closely followed by The Rolling Stones and other groups. Performers nowadays regarded as icons such as Bob Dylan and Jerry Lee Lewis appeared, as later did Pink Floyd, Led Zeppelin and Genesis, while the finale of the city's first Rhythm and Blues Festival featured a new vocalist by the name of Rod Stewart. The movement popularly known as Brum Beat consisted of several local groups setting out on the road to stardom: these included Carl Wayne and The Vikings, The Move and The Moody Blues. Some of these startling (at the time) developments are brought to life on the pages that follow, but it was the sheer range and variety of entertainment available that cannot be properly conveyed: folksong concerts; concerts of Scottish music, Irish music, Polish music, Asian music; Jugoslav and Greek dancers; Welsh choirs; the Bands of the Royal Marines and the Grenadier Guards, the Joe Loss, Glenn Miller, Woody Herman and Edmundo Ros Orchestras, the Vienna Boys Choir, the Jacques Loussier Trio, Ravi Shankar, The Swingle Singers and comedians Victoria Wood, Max Boyce and Jasper Carrott.

On a rather more staid front was a 'Fashion and Beauty Show' in 1962 fronted by Royal designer Norman Hartnell, while 1964 saw two singular visitors arrive to give speeches: one was Harold Wilson, who chose Birmingham to launch his 1964 election campaign, and the other Mary Whitehouse, whose 'Clean Up TV Campaign' began in Birmingham and drew her supporters from across the country to pack the Town Hall.

RIGHT All-night jazz under threat in 1961 – the banner reads 'Don't Ban the Ball'.

BELOW RIGHT All-night jazz takes its toll.

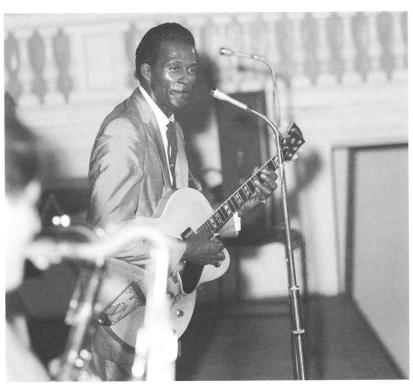

LEFT
1962: the city's first
rock 'n' twist night.

BELOW LEFT
Chuck Berry
commands the
stage.

Cliff Richard enjoying his fan mail.

ABOVE The Beatles
soon found disguises
necessary.

LEFT   The Rolling
Stones giving
'satisfaction'.

RIGHT One of the most influential rock
and rollers of the time, Little Richard.

BELOW Manfred Mann arrive
at Elmdon (now Birmingham
International) Airport.

Carl Wayne & The Vikings
(LEFT) and the Moody Blues
(BELOW) were part of the
60s Brum Beat era.

RIGHT The Spencer Davis Group
were formed in Birmingham.

BELOW Bob Dylan included
Birmingham on his first
UK tour in 1965.

© Daniel Kramer

ABOVE
1969: Tour by 'Delaney and Bonnie and Friends', the 'friends' being Eric Clapton (left) and George Harrison (right).

LEFT 1968: Simon and Garfunkel play the Town Hall.

ABOVE
1961: theatrical goings-on
show the versatility of the
Town Hall.

LEFT The Town Hall takes a leading role in the 1967 film *Privilege* starring Jean Shrimpton and Manfred Mann's Paul Jones.

BELOW The spirit of the 1920s is revived at a 'Roaring Twenties Ball' in 1967.

RIGHT Proud moment for a youngster showing a model of his parish church to the Bishop of Birmingham, The Rt Rev Leonard Wilson.

BELOW
1965: the jostle at the tea bar was part of the ritual of Town Hall concert going for many decades.

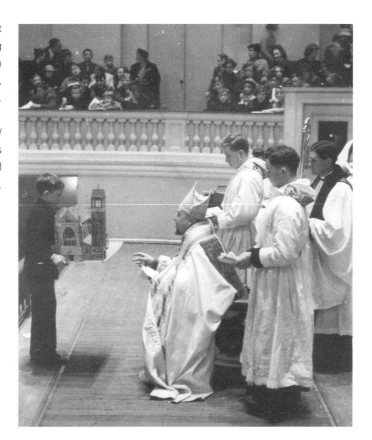

TOP Principal Conductor Hugo Rignold (1960-68) with the CBSO.

LEFT Guest conductor Rafael Frühbeck de Burgos and (ABOVE) Constantin Silvestri.

RIGHT Elisabeth
Schwarzkopf was
one of the first
international artists
to appear in the
recital series
sponsored by
Birmingham's
Reginald Vincent.

BELOW The CBSO's
dynamic Louis
Frémaux (1969–78).

VINCENT'S PRESENT

CELEBRITY CONCERT No. 5

TOWN HALL, BIRMINGHAM
TUESDAY, 17th OCTOBER, 1967
at 7.30 p.m.

THE RADIANT VOICE OF

ELISABETH SCHWARZKOPF

with

GEOFFREY PARSONS — piano

Photo: Fayer, Vien

Songs by BACH, GLUCK, HANDEL, MOZART, SCHUMANN, MAHLER, WOLF, MOUSSORGSKY, TCHAIKOVSKY, RACHMANINOV and STRAVINSKY.

Tickets 25/- 20/- 15/- 12/6 10/- 7/6
ON SALE NOW FROM VINCENT'S, 11 NEEDLESS ALLEY, BIRMINGHAM 2 (MID. 2207)
AND FROM OCTOBER 3rd AT THE TOWN HALL BOX OFFICE (CEN. 2392)

Printed by Husband & Currell Ltd., 240 Holliday Street, Birmingham 1.

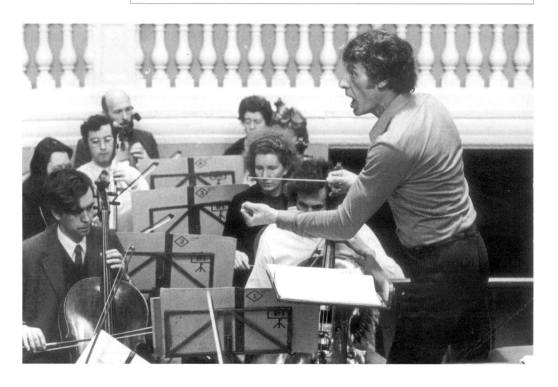

ABOVE Popular CBSO conductor Harold Gray makes a 'Last Night of the Proms' speech.

LEFT
Andrzej Panufnik, CBSO Conductor (1957–9) with CBSO Leader Felix Kok (1965–88).

RIGHT A familiar face in the 60s and 70s, the French cellist Paul Tortelier.

BELOW André Previn rehearses the London Symphony Orchestra.

LEFT Music while you work: one of the Town Hall staff is serenaded by Birmingham Secondary Schools pupils in 1974.

BELOW
Queen Victoria surveys her subjects.

The Town Hall in summer and winter. RIGHT Note the open space (foreground) where Galloways' Corner stood until it was demolished in 1970.

LEFT
1974: The Rt Hon Edward Heath on the campaign trail.

BELOW 1979: The first CBI Conference to be held in Birmingham.

RIGHT Elton John tries his
hand as a DJ at a
Birmingham radio station.

BELOW 1973: Status Quo.

LEFT David Bowie toured as Ziggy Stardust in 1972 and 1973.

BELOW Bay City Rollers.

© Robert Ellis/Repfoto

Birmingham has been described as the birthplace of Heavy Metal with Black Sabbath (TOP), Judas Priest and Led Zeppelin (ABOVE) all coming from the Midlands.

ABOVE 1975:
Another famous
Birmingham band,
ELO (Electric Light
Orchestra).

LEFT Queen's
legendary
Freddie Mercury.

RIGHT Fairport
Convention's
Dave Swarbrick and
Dave Pegg
(back row).

CURTAIN DOWN – FOR THE MOMENT

AT THE BEGINNING OF THE 1980S few would even have dreamed that before the decade was out a new concert hall would be under construction in Birmingham. Much talked of during the greater part of the century, it had occasionally even been forecast, but when in 1986 Jacques Delors, President of the European Commission, laid the foundation stone of the new building that would house Symphony Hall there were few, if any, who recalled the well-intentioned promise of a new concert hall that Neville Chamberlain had made almost sixty years before. Instead the venerable old Town Hall had continued its faithful service to the citizens of Birmingham, meeting the needs of each new decade and each turn of taste and fashion with stoic fortitude.

Yet over the next 15 years it was to witness even more excitements, especially on the musical front. Who could have forecast, for instance, that at the beginning of the 1980s the tenth conductor in the 60-year history of the CBSO would be a 25-year-old, and that Simon Rattle would stay beyond the date in 1996 when the Town Hall would (temporarily) put up its shutters? Or that when in March 1982 city organist Sir George Thalben-Ball gave his 900th organ recital (at the age of 86) and retired soon afterwards, his successor would be another 25-year old, Thomas Trotter? (Remarkably, there have been only four previous organists in all the years since James Stimpson was appointed in 1842, with each of his successors serving not less than 25 years.) An important anniversary that loomed in the 1980s was the Hall's 150th, appropriately celebrated by a performance of Elgar's choral work *The Music Makers,* 72 years after the composer had stood on the same platform to direct its première during the last of the old triennial festivals.

Birmingham's proud record in music education work for young people continued on with schools concerts; military bands played and, with the Hall's doors firmly closed, the CBSO undertook the largest commercial recording project the building had ever witnessed when it made a set of all Beethoven's nine symphonies (followed up later by the five piano concertos). In 1990, however, the doors were firmly open to admit a spectacle not previously seen:

boxing. No greater contrast could be drawn than with the annual Remembrance Day services which dignified the building each November. And between 1988-90 the annual ceremony of mayor-making moved from the Council House to the Town Hall so that the public could attend. During these years a clutch of national politicians including Margaret Thatcher, Neil Kinnock, Roy Jenkins and Tony Benn were to be heard, and personalities such as the astrologer Patrick Moore and yachtsman Chay Blyth all appeared. It was business as usual, as it always had been; and even when Symphony Hall opened in 1991 in a blaze of publicity its elderly neighbour simply carried on with its work. It even doubled as London's Royal Albert Hall in the popular film 'Brassed Off'. The CBSO's final concert had taken place on 16 May 1991, but other concerts and public attractions kept it going for another five years until the decision was made to bring down the curtain. On 12 July 1996 a special concert marked by goodwill messages that nevertheless looked forward confidently to the Town Hall's reappearance at some future date signalled the actual closure.

And so it was entertainment, of one sort or another, to the last, whether the latest popular crowd-pulling sensation such as UB40, David Essex or Gary Numan, comedians Frank Skinner, Jo Brand and Lenny Henry, or great international orchestras such as the Leipzig Gewandhaus or the Amsterdam Concertgebouw paying the city return visits. The distinguished Austrian maestro Willi Boskovsky arrived from Vienna, and was disbelieving when assured that he had played in the Town Hall as a member of the Vienna Philharmonic Orchestra in 1935; now he led Strauss waltzes from the violin just as Johann Strauss himself had done on the same platform 143 years before.

In one respect, at least, nothing had changed.

150th Anniversary of the Town Hall

Saturday 6th October 1984

NATIONAL ANTHEM
contralto: Alfreda Hodgson
arr. Elgar

OVERTURE, THE CONSECRATION OF THE HOUSE

ORGAN CONCERTO
organ: Thomas Trotter
Poulenc

Interval
A warning bell will be sounded five minutes before the end of the Interval

ORGAN SYMPHONY No.5 (excerpts)
organ: Thomas Trotter
Widor

THE MUSIC MAKERS
contralto: Alfreda Hodgson
Elgar

City of Birmingham Symphony Orchestra
Conductor, Simon Rattle
Leader, Felix Kok
CBSO Chorus, Chorus Master Simon Halsey

A celebration marked the 150th anniversary
of the Town Hall in 1984.
View from the Upper Gallery (BELOW).

LEFT Among the guests was former City Organist Sir George Thalben-Ball with Thomas Trotter.

BELOW LEFT Sir George Thalben-Ball, City Organist (1949–83).

BELOW Thomas Trotter, City Organist (1983–)

ABOVE
Willi Boskovsky's
regular programmes
of music by the
Viennese Strauss
family were always
immensely popular.

RIGHT The City of
Birmingham Choir,
founded in 1921,
introduced annual
carol concerts which
ran throughout the
1980s up to the Hall's
closure. Conductor,
Christopher Robinson.

Birmingham
continued to attract
the greatest names
in classical music
such as the
conductors Claudio
Abbado (LEFT) and
Bernard Haitink
(BELOW).

LEFT
1986: Nigel
Kennedy playing
hard.

BELOW
1988: The CBSO
and Chorus with
Walter Weller
recording
Beethoven's *Choral*
Symphony.

ABOVE
1985: Bernard Herrmann conducts the Birmingham Schools Concert Orchestra. Such concerts gave many young people their first experience of the Town Hall – and of music.

LEFT
Victor Borge, the Danish comic maestro up to his familiar tricks.

RIGHT
1987: soundcheck for a David
Essex concert.

BELOW
Birmingham's UB40 were
among the big names.

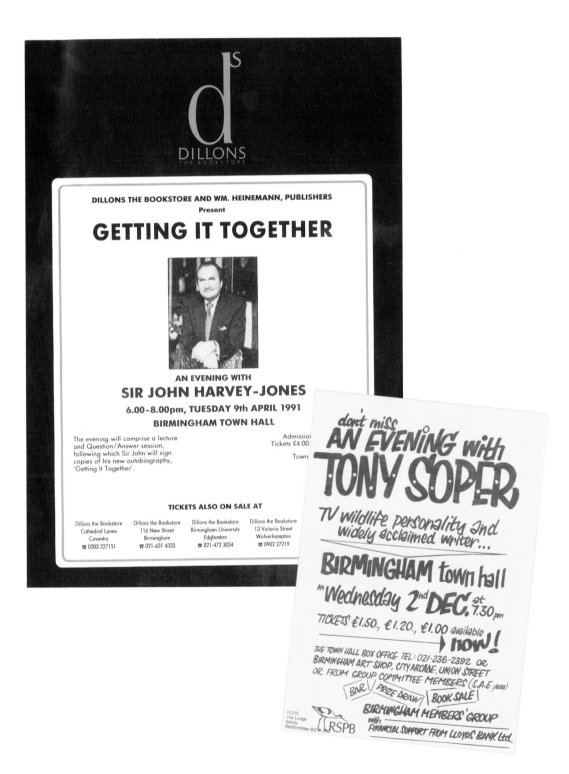

ds
DILLONS
THE BOOKSTORE

DILLONS THE BOOKSTORE AND WM. HEINEMANN, PUBLISHERS
Present

GETTING IT TOGETHER

AN EVENING WITH
SIR JOHN HARVEY-JONES
6.00–8.00pm, TUESDAY 9th APRIL 1991
BIRMINGHAM TOWN HALL

The evening will comprise a lecture
and Question/Answer session,
following which Sir John will sign
copies of his new autobiography,
'Getting It Together'.

Admission
Tickets £4.00

Town

TICKETS ALSO ON SALE AT

Dillons the Bookstore
Cathedral Lanes
Coventry
☎ 0203 227151

Dillons the Bookstore
116 New Street
Birmingham
☎ 021-631 4333

Dillons the Bookstore
Birmingham University
Edgbaston
☎ 021-472 3034

Dillons the Bookstore
13 Victoria Street
Wolverhampton
☎ 0902 27219

don't miss
AN EVENING with
TONY SOPER
TV wildlife personality and
widely acclaimed writer...

BIRMINGHAM town hall
on Wednesday 2nd DEC. at 7.30pm

TICKETS £1.50, £1.20., £1.00 available
▶ now!

THE TOWN HALL BOX OFFICE TEL: 021-236-2392 OR
BIRMINGHAM ART SHOP, CITY ARCADE, UNION STREET
OR FROM GROUP COMMITTEE MEMBERS (S.A.E please)
BAR / PRIZE DRAW / BOOK SALE
BIRMINGHAM MEMBERS' GROUP
with
FINANCIAL SUPPORT FROM LLOYDS BANK Ltd.

RSPB
The Lodge
Sandy
Bedfordshire SG19 2DL
RSPB

ABOVE
1990: Councillor (Sir) Bernard Zissman is installed as Lord Mayor. Between 1988–90 the annual ceremony was moved to the Town Hall so that the public could attend.

RIGHT
Freemasons had gathered at the Town Hall since 1928.

ABOVE Saying goodbye: The CBSO and Simon Rattle at one of their final Town Hall concerts in 1991.

LEFT Full complement of Town Hall staff at the CBSO's last concert, with manager Betty Milne (third row centre, black jacket).

EPILOGUE   After the Town Hall shut its doors in 1996, a £35m funding package from Birmingham City Council, Heritage Lottery Fund and European Regional Development Fund enabled renovation work to commence in 2005. A team of conservation and construction experts, led by Urban Design, Rodney Melville and Partners and Wates Construction began the painstaking task of repairing the building. A quarry in Anglesey was opened in order to provide stone as close to the original as possible and 40 stonemasons and carvers have been involved in the repairs. The lead roof has been replaced and the internal shape of the main hall restored to the single balcony configuration of 1834. Intricate plasterwork has been repaired and the beautiful ceiling designs restored to their former glory. Improvements to access have been made to both front and back of house including the provision of lifts. Acoustic treatment has been

applied to the windows, an acoustic canopy and sophisticated technical equipment installed to ensure the building's future as a flexible venue for the 21st century.

This much-loved landmark has now been restored to its rightful place at the heart of Birmingham's cultural life, a place for entertainment, civic and public functions, welcoming back the people of Birmingham to what is believed to be the oldest remaining purpose-built concert hall in the world.

LEFT
A last look at the old Town Hall.

Urban Design

LEFT The 1927
gallery is demolished.

BELOW A rare
close-up of the
intricate plasterwork.

RIGHT A web of scaffolding.

BELOW 2007: Town Hall Birmingham.